The Adventures of Tommy Trucker and His Best Friend Jack

The Load of Jelly Beans

Bonus Story

The Load of Cheese Popcorn

Author

Rosalee J Pierce

Editing and some Illustrations by Rosalee J Pierce

All road photos taken by Eric R Pierce

Jack is a rescue dog from Mount Eagle Tennessee. A nice man found him walking out of the woods starved and full of ticks. He took him to the Vet and fixed him up. Tommy Trucker came along and adopted him.

This book is dedicated to the many animal rescue missions, shelters, shelter workers and foster families as well as the transporters who help make it all happen. Thank you for having a heart.

A special thanks goes out to Paige Nordstrom for designing this book cover as well as the illustrations on page 13,14, and 16. She also designed the illustration on page 37 of the bonus story. Paige is currently an Art Student in Green Bay, Wisconisn. She is very talented, Eric and I are blessed to have her be part of our book projects.

Just as Tommy was filling his thermos with coffee at the truck stop, he overheard some other truckers talking about a dog out in the parking lot going bonkers in the driver's seat. *Oh no, I hope that's not Jack.* Tommy thought to himself as he hurried to the counter to pay for his coffee.

Tommy ran out into the parking lot. Yep, it was Jack pulling the air horn with his teeth Wahh Wahh it sounded. Jack was barking nonstop. "Oh no how embarrassing" Tommy mumbled as he climbed into his truck.

What's the matter boy? Calm down" said Tommy to Jack who sat there panting in the passenger seat. Then Tommy heard the load alarm go off on his computer Beep! Beep! It sounded.

Tommy turned up the volume on the CB radio as some truckers were talking about him. Tommy grabbed the CB mike and said, "Yes it was my dog going bonkers. He always does that when the load alarm goes off, he's a true trucking dog." Replied Tommy.

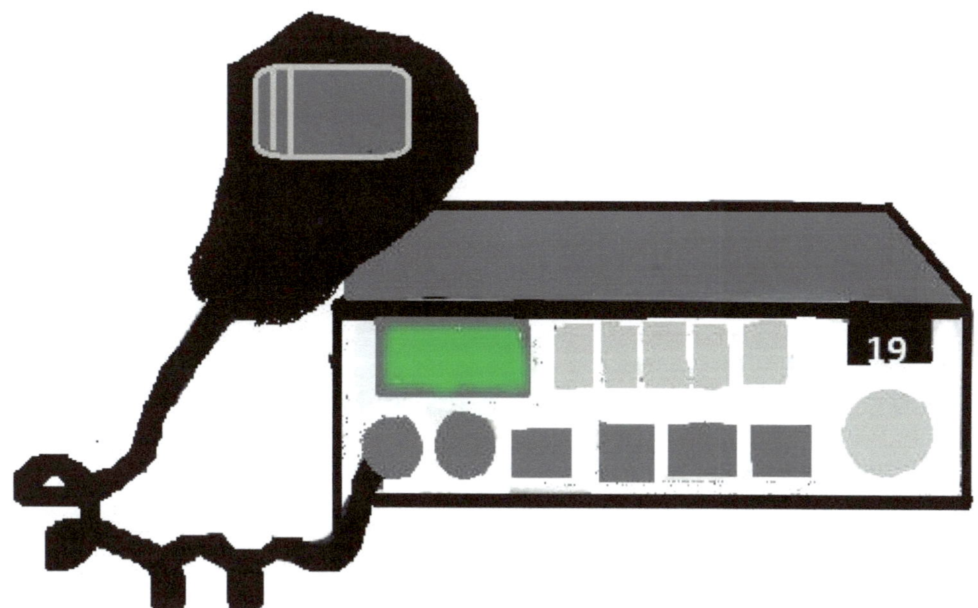

Tommy pushed a few buttons on his computer, "let's see where this one goes."

Tommy pushed a few more buttons on his computer and looked at Jack. "This load picks up in Ohio and delivers in Kentucky. It looks like 40,000 (forty thousand) pounds of Jelly Beans." Jack's head tilted as he heard the words "Jelly Beans". *After all, those are the yummiest candies in the whole world* thought Jack.

"Let's go for a walk before we head out" Tommy said. He popped open the passenger door and hooked Jack's leash onto his collar. They walked over to the row of trees lining the parking lot. A few trucks drove passed and waved at the two truckers as they walked around.

"You know Jack, you really embarrassed me back there" Tommy stated to Jack as they got back on the road heading toward the Jelly Bean factory. Jack just put his head down and jumped on the bed to relax while Tommy turned on the radio to listen to some music.

        Down the road, the two traveled until they made the final turn into the guard shack. "Hello sir, I'm here for a load to Kentucky. Here's my pick up number" Tommy said to the Guard at the gate. "Put it in door number 4 driver" said the Guard as he pushed the button to release the gate.

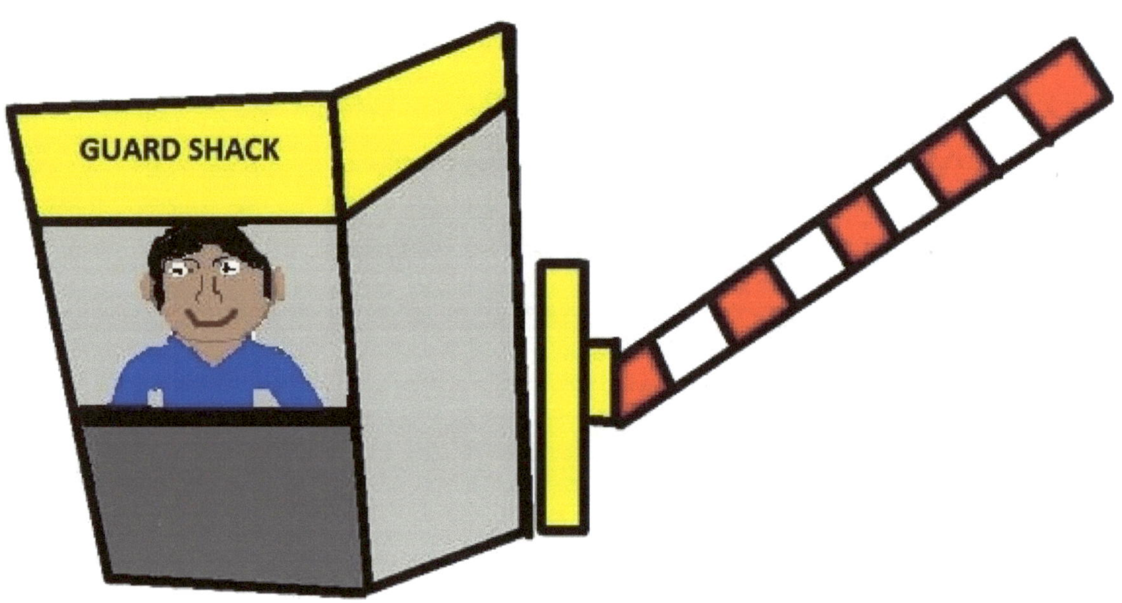

Tommy wheeled his big rig so he could back up into door number 4. Jack got off the bed and jumped up on the passenger seat to watch. "This place makes Jelly Beans boy, if you're good maybe we'll get some for the trip to share" whispered Tommy into Jacks ear.

As the workers were loading Tommy's trailer, Tommy walked back to adjust the refrigerated unit to 50 degrees. By doing that, the Jelly Beans wouldn't be too soft or too hard when he delivered them.

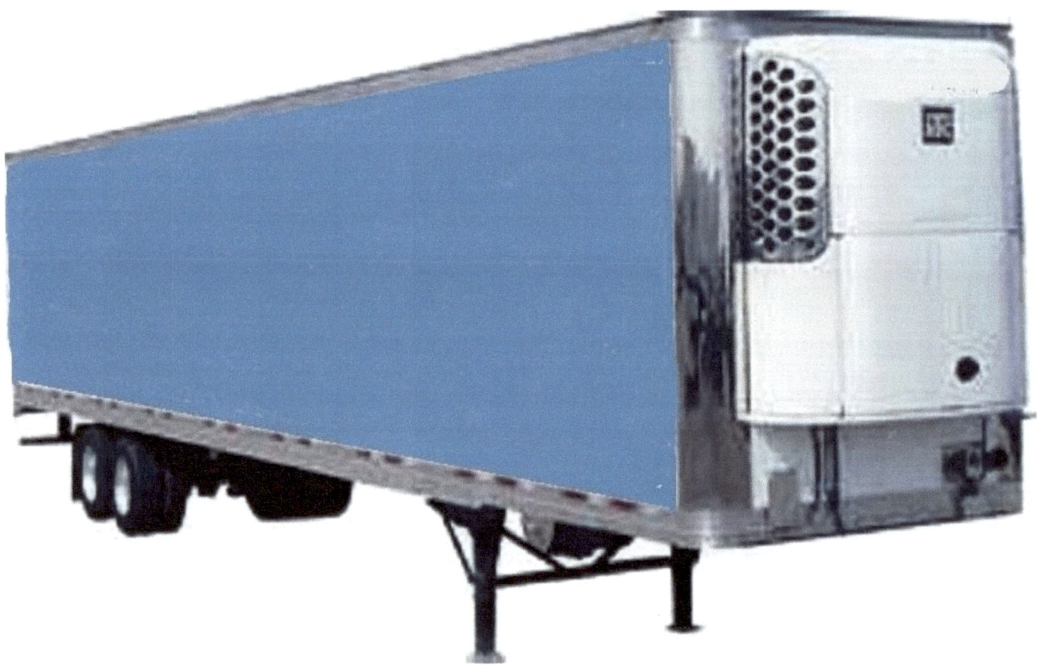

One problem though, Tommy left the truck door open. Jack jumped out and nose to the ground followed the Jelly Bean smell right through an open door and onto the factory floor!

Oh the smells! Thought Jack. Big machines stirring and pouring the Jelly Bean mixture into yet another machine to form the little bean shapes coated with a magical flavoring of the rainbow. Cherry, grape, lemon, lime, orange just to name a few.

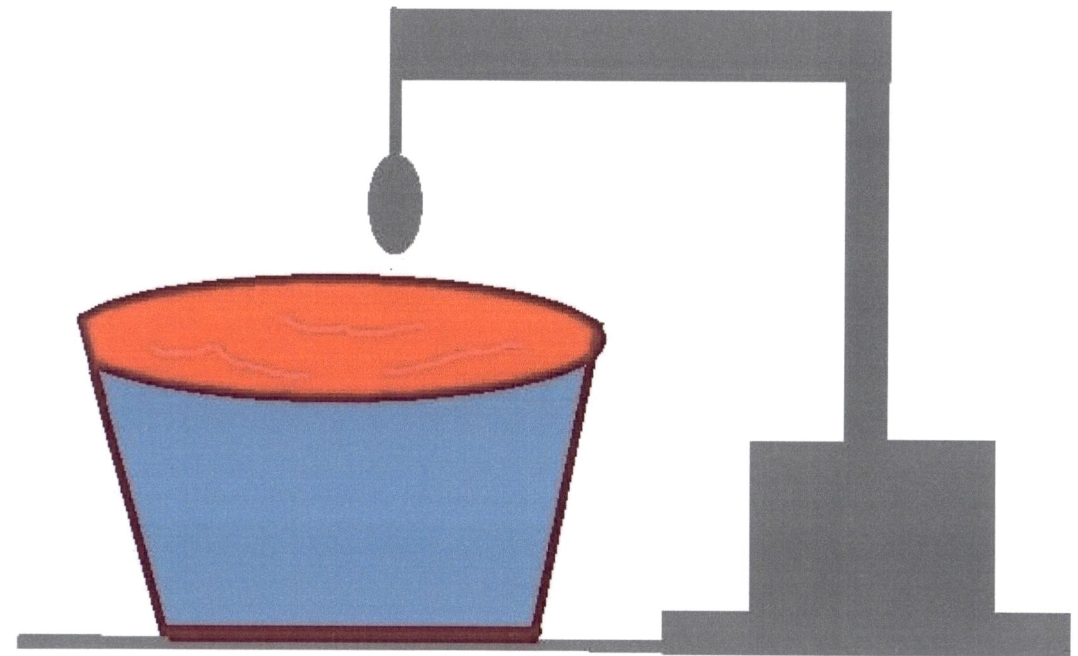

Jack ran under the conveyor that transported all the candies down to be put into packages. *Hey look there's some on the floor!* Thought Jack. He gobbled those up and as he swallowed the last one off the floor he looked up to find a man with a hairnet in a white coat staring at him and he didn't look happy.

Meanwhile at the dock, Tommy was searching all over for his furry friend. Then, someone pulled the emergency alarm. Tommy heard that and knew Jack had something to do with it.

"Come here little doggie" said the man in the hairnet. He reached for Jacks collar. Jack noticed packages of Jelly Beans on a long table to be boxed up. He tucked his tail between his legs, put his head down and ran under the man's legs to get away. Jack grabbed a bag of beans and headed out the door as fast as he could.

"Get him!" shouted the men in the white coats. The next thing Jack knew there were six or seven people with hairnets all chasing him out of the building!

Tommy arrived at the packaging table and followed the crowd of hairnets and white coats out of the building. Jack ran around the corner of the building and hid under another man's truck and trailer with the bag of Jelly Beans in his mouth.

As Jack ran back to Tommy's truck, there was another problem. There was a hole in the bag and it was leaking a trail of Jelly Beans right to Jack's hiding spot. Jack didn't know this, so he jumped back up into Tommy's truck with his bag of beans.

Tommy, along with the crowd of workers, followed the trail of candy to find Jack lying on the bed in Tommy's truck chomping on what Jelly Beans were left in the bag. "There you are, what did you do?" Tommy shouted waving his finger.

The men with the hairnets stood in a group and decided he did nothing wrong other than steal a bag of candy. As long as Tommy paid for the bag of Jelly Beans Jack stole, they would all go back to work and finish loading his truck.

"Thank you so much and here's the money for the bag of Jelly Beans Jack took off the table" said Tommy. He handed the men some money to cover the price of the candy. "I'm very sorry guys, I don't know why he behaved like that" stated Tommy to the men in the hairnets.

Tommy's trailer was loaded quickly to get him on his way. Tommy and Jack drove out of there as fast as they could. A few miles down the road, Tommy heard whimpering and smelled a big cloud of stink coming from Tommy's bed. It was Jack. He had a tummy ache because he ate too many Jelly Beans. "Oh great, you did it to yourself you mooching pooch" said Tommy. Just then, he pulled over into the nearest rest area to let Jack outside.

He couldn't get the door open fast enough for Jack. The dog ran outside before Tommy could get his leash on him. After about half an hour they were back on the road traveling to Kentucky to deliver those Jelly Beans. Tommy made his way out of Ohio and into Indiana.

There was some chatter on the CB about a pick- up truck that lost its load of tires and they ended up all over the highway making a big mess.

Tommy grabbed the mike and asked "break one nine, what's the twenty on the tires? Forget it, I found them" said Tommy as he drove around a curve. A Trucker responded, "The pick-up got towed and the tires are spread out all over highway 65 southbound by exit 47" *This is just a bad day, I'm having a bad day* Thought Tommy.

There was a tow truck there getting ready to tow the pickup truck away. There were lights flashing from the police who were directing traffic and from the tow truck leaving the scene. The road was littered with old tires as the highway was at a standstill. Tommy set the brakes to wait in the traffic jam with the other trucks.

All those trucks were loaded with some type of product. They could have hot dogs, or potato chips or maybe toy cars or basket balls, bicycles or televisions. They all had something in their trailers waiting to be delivered. No one was going anywhere. The chatter on the CB radio was loud as the truckers were complaining about the guy who loaded his pickup too heavy with old tires.

Jack woke up from his nap and was getting wiggly. "Well hello boy, as soon as we can, we'll stop so you can stretch your legs" said Tommy to Jack. They found a truck stop up ahead and pulled into the fuel lane. "We've got a few minutes to wait so let's walk over to those trees" said Tommy.

Jack began sniffing the ground, it started to rain a little then quickly turned heavy like it was raining cats and dogs! The two Truckers ran back to the truck to get some fuel. Jack shook the rain off of his back then climbed up the ramp into the truck.

Tommy wheeled his big rig to a nice parking spot in the back row to park for the evening. "We'll stop here for the night and head out early in the morning" said Tommy. He told Jack the plan for the night as he climbed back into the sleeper part of the truck to straighten the bed and to see if Jack made a mess on the blanket.

Tommy filled Jack's water bowl and gave him a pat on the head. "I should have known you were going to get into trouble today, as soon as I said the words Jelly Beans. Even before we got to the factory I sensed you had a plan" Tommy said. He pets him on his head and rubbed his achy belly. "I'm going into the restaurant for a bite to eat boy, I think you should just drink some water and rest at this point. I will be back, hope you feel better." Tommy locked up the truck, but kept the engine running. Big rigs are meant to run and Jack needed to keep warm, so Tommy left the heat on for him.

Tommy sat down at a booth in the restaurant and ordered a dinner plate special. A waitress named Melissa asked him how his trip was going. "I'm not sure you have the time to hear this" said Tommy. "It's slow right now sir, what happened?" questioned Melissa.

Tommy told her about how his day started with Jack going bonkers. Then, he told her about what happened at the factory. The two sat there and laughed at what Jack had done. "Order up" said the cook. "It Looks like your dinner is ready" said Melissa. She brought it over to Tommy and re-filled his coffee.

Melissa went into the gift shop to buy a small bag of Jelly Beans as a joke and placed a handful on Tommy's plate. "Here's your dessert sir, on the house" Melissa said to Tommy with a smile. Tommy just looked up, shook his head and laughed.

Tommy came back to the truck to get ready for bed. Jack was drooling on Tommy's favorite pillow. Tommy brushed his teeth in his sink and washed his face. As Tommy lay in bed he thought about how boring his life would be if he didn't have Jack to ride with him. Then he drifted off to sleep.

The next morning came so fast it seemed like they just fell asleep. Tommy woke up before the alarm went off, so he quickly pushed the button to shut it off. Tommy pulled on his boots and combed his hair quick before Jack woke up. He popped open the door and called for Jack.

Jack sat in the passenger seat and was quiet for most of the ride. It had rained the night before and the roads were wet. The two traveled through Louisville, Kentucky with no problems as the weather was dry. It was early spring in the city. "Look at the dinosaur he's going to get you!" laughed Tommy. Jack started to growl at the statue on the side of the road. Tommy laughed some more as the two Truckers traveled down the road.

Down the highway they went with forty thousand (40,000) pounds of Jelly Beans loaded in the trailer on their way to the store shelves. There were red ones, green ones and yellow ones. They were all mixed up together in bags just waiting to be popped open and poured into candy dishes.

Just then an oversized truck pulling the base of a windmill was in front of Tommy driving real slow. Tommy turned on his turn signal to change lanes to get ready to pass. "Wow that will be a big windmill once they put it all together" Jack just sat in the passenger seat with his window partially down. Jack didn't care, he was still trying to feel better after eating all those Jelly Beans.

"Look there's a windfarm now" said Tommy.

27

The two arrived at their delivery place on time. As the dock workers unloaded Tommy's trailer, He pushed a few buttons on his computer to tell Sarah in the office his trailer was empty and he's ready for another load.

Tommy took the rug that was on the floor outside to shake it out. He wanted to get rid of some dog hair. On the dash was the bag of Jelly Beans Melissa the waitress gave to him. He picked up a red one for Jack. The pup licked Tommy's wrist and gently took the treat from Tommy. "I still love you even if you are trouble sometimes." Tommy gave Jack a kiss on his head and said "I wonder where we'll go next?"

The End

The Load of Cheese Popcorn

Author

Rosalee J Pierce

Tommy picked up the soccer ball and tossed it to Jack one more time. Jack jumped up high into the air to try and catch it but, it bounced off his nose and rolled over by a tree. Meanwhile, Tommy took his handkerchief out from his back pocket to wipe the slobber off of his hands from the slobbered up soccer ball

Ding a ling, ding a ling went Tommy's phone in his pocket. "Oh hang on caller, I'll be right with you" said Tommy as he fumbled with his handkerchief trying to dry his hands. The caller was his Broker Sam telling Tommy about a load going back to Green Bay, Wisconsin.

"You say it picks up on my way back north? I should just start heading for home and it's on the way? That's great Sam, will it pay for my fuel and maybe a new handkerchief?" asked Tommy as he chuckled and decided not to stuff it back into his pants pocket.

"Yep, this one will not only pay for your fuel Tommy, it will buy you and your wife a nice steak dinner when you get home" replied Sam the Broker. A Broker is someone who finds loads for truck drivers to fill their trailers.

"I'll do it Sam, send the load information to the truck please" said Tommy to Sam. Just then, Tommy whistled for Jack but he was busy starring at a red tailed squirrel who was busy digging for an acorn to munch on. "Come on boy, we're going home for the weekend!" shouted Tommy. Jack caught the word "home" and forgot all about the squirrel and his nut. Jack picked up his soccer ball and trotted towards the truck.

Tommy pulled out the new ramp he bought for Jack to get in and out of the truck easier it fits nicely behind the cab with a couple of tie down straps. Tommy pulled his new ramp out and Jack climbed up with no trouble he didn't even drop his soccer ball.

Tommy read the load information trying to see what type of product it was so he knew what he was dealing with. *I hope it's not potato chips, a driver can't take those over the mountains as the bags sometimes pop open due to the higher elevation levels* Tommy thought to himself. "Here it is, oh boy Jack you'd better make sure you behave yourself on this load" stated Tommy to Jack. You see, it was a load of popcorn. It was 6 skids of caramel corn, 6 skids of butter flavored, and 10 skids of cheese popcorn.

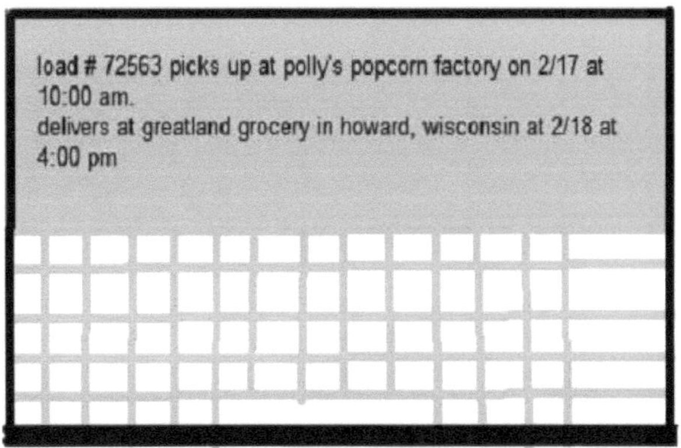

There are three things in this world that Jack just can't resist. They are jelly beans, breaded chicken pieces, and any kind of popcorn. Tommy bent over to whisper in Jacks ear what the product was. "It's a load of popcorn" whispered Tommy.

Jacks ears perked up and his eyes got big, his tail started to wag uncontrollably. "You promise me you will be nice" warned Tommy as he made Jack shake his paw on the deal. "This picks up at 10:00 am. Then it delivers to that big huge grocery store that is off the highway near our house where we sometimes buy your dog food" stated Tommy to his best but sometimes naughty friend.

Since the "P" word had been spoken, Jack was already drooling as he thought about the delicious cheese they sprinkle on the perfectly popped corn. *Those guys really know what they are doing at that factory* thought Jack as he had been there before when he was really little but, he still remembers the smells.

He climbed up in the passenger seat to get ready for the ride and sniffed a few sniffs out of the window. Tommy started the truck engine, Varooooom it sounded. "Let me fix your blanket and fill your water dish to get ready for the ride boy" said Tommy as he climbed out of the truck to shake some dog hair off the blanket. "Ok let's get rolling!" as he put the truck into gear, they slowly made their way out of the rest area where they were playing ball.

The two truckers rode along for about an hour or so when they came to their exit to get off the highway. "Ok, our pick up spot is at this exit you remember to be nice" warned Tommy again.

Tommy wheeled his big rig through the intersection and down the street to pick up his load of popcorn. Stopping at the Guard shack he handed the man the load information. The guard told Tommy to back up to dock door number 3.

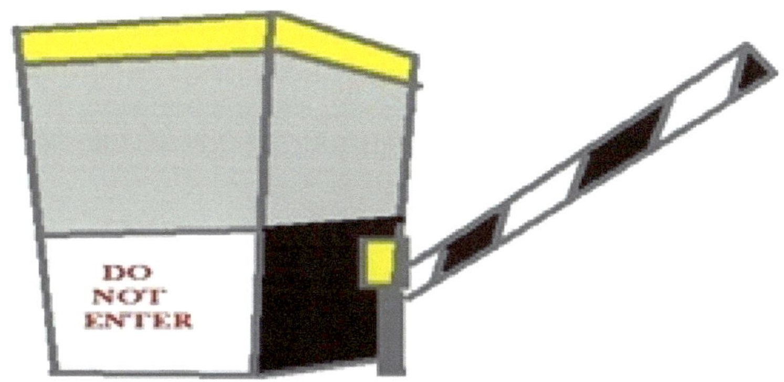

This door was right across from a large pond with ducks swimming in it. Whoosh went the air brakes, and Tommy climbed out of this truck to pull out Jacks ramp. "Lets' go for a walk boy, they've got a few trucks ahead of us, it may be a while" said Tommy to Jack.

The two walked over to the pond to check things out. There were baby ducks swimming in a small group. "I don't see any mama ducks or daddy ducks anywhere. I don't even see a grandpa or a grandma duck. I wonder who is taking care of them" said Tommy.

The pup started to sniff the ground he pulled Tommy along the shore of the pond then plopped down and started to roll around. "Oh no you don't we don't need that duck poop smelling up the truck" shouted Tommy as he yanked on the leash. "Geez that's all we need" mumbled Tommy. "Once we get loaded this is a non-stop flight to Green Bay. We're not stopping to eat we'll eat what we packed in the truck. The only thing we'll stop for is to use the potty in your case, a tree and that's it" stated Tommy to his furry friend.

The two began to walk back to the truck, Jack started to whine and pull on his leash to go back to the pond. "Don't worry about those ducks we'll find something to feed them before we leave" said Tommy.

The air smelled like popcorn, Jack stuck his nose up to get a good sniff as he walked with Tommy on his leash. Just then, another man started to wave at Tommy. "Hey Tommy, how are you?" said the other Trucker. "Hey Jim, fancy meeting you here" replied Tommy. The two men stood in front of Tommy's truck and talked about the good ole' days while Jack sat down to watch the forklift driver load their trailer. "Thank goodness the price of fuel went down a little" said Jim.

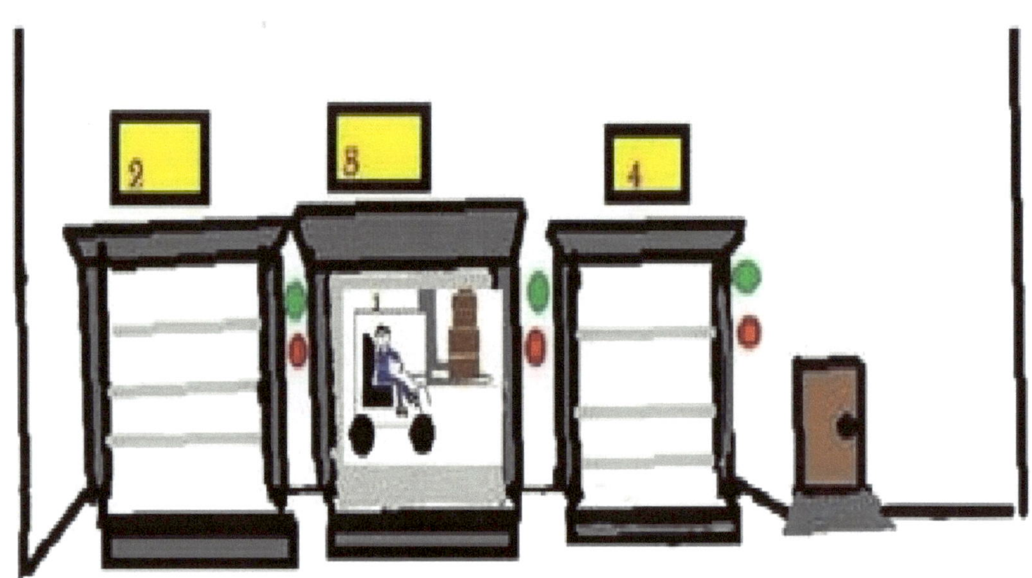

"I know it was getting harder to make my truck payment. Now that it's gone down I'm going to visit the CB shop when I get home and buy me a new CB that's top shelf, wall to wall tree top tall!" laughed Tommy. The two men laughed and joked around.

All of a sudden there was a loud KABOOOM! Everyone stopped to look but, it was just the forklift driver, he dropped a skid of popcorn and a couple boxes had busted open.

Tommy and Jim went back to talking but Jack couldn't help but notice that there was a bag open on the dock floor and it was the cheese kind!

Just then, Jack wiggled out of his collar and bounded up the stairs to the loading zone to fetch himself a bag of cheese popcorn! He took his little front pincher teeth and dragged the bag back down the steps. *I must be nice I must be nice* thought Jack. He dragged the open bag of cheese popcorn across the parking lot and over to the pond to feed those baby ducks!

Jack thought *this is nice Tommy will be happy.* He took the bag and shook it into the water. He of course ate a mouthful for himself then shook the bag again into the water for the baby ducks. Soon, the babies swam over to the edge of the pond to see what was floating in the water. Jacks nose was covered in cheese.

Suddenly, Jack noticed out of the corner of his eye the forklift driver trying to sneak up on him! The pup ran as fast as he could while still carrying the ripped bag of cheese popcorn. Jack ran over by a tree and stopped suddenly into a pile of duck poop. The forklift driver slipped "Oh no!" he shouted. He landed flat on his back into some piles of duck poop! It was all over his jacket and in his hair, gross!

"I'm going to get you dog" warned the forklift driver. Jack just sat under the tree, he dropped the bag on the ground and sat there panting. "Come look at what your dog did Tommy!" shouted the forklift driver. Just then, Tommy and Jim ran over to the pond with Jacks collar and placed it back around his neck. "What did you do now? I asked you to be nice boy and now look at this poor guy he's covered in duck poop!" shouted Tommy to Jack.

"I hope this covers the price of a new jacket, I'm really sorry" said Tommy. He reached into his wallet and pulled out $60.00 dollars. "Oh it might" moaned the forklift driver as he rolled over and got back up on his feet.

Jack quickly ate a couple more mouthfuls of cheese popcorn before someone took the bag away. Tommy took the bag and shook the last bit into the water for the ducks. "You come with me, you stink and are getting a bath right now! Even if I have to take you through a car wash! Shouted Tommy to Jack.

The forklift driver took off his jacket and balled it up to toss it into the trash. "You don't have to do that, there's a pet store down the road that has a groomer she'll have him smelling like a flower in no time" he said laughing. "Good idea, thanks" replied Tommy.

"You're loaded by the way, pick up your papers at the Guard shack" said the forklift driver. "Thanks guy, I'm really sorry my pup has a heart as big as Texas and is always worried about other animals" said Tommy. "We feed those baby ducks every morning, they are well taken care of" replied the forklift driver.

With a smile, the two men shook hands. Tommy started his truck Varoom went the engine. Jack was loaded up in the truck and was told not to step one foot on that bed or he would be left at home next trip.

Tommy made his way down the road to find the pet store that has a groomer to give Jack a bath. "You stink, and you're smelling up my truck" said Tommy to Jack. He unhooked the ramp to let Jack out. As the two truckers entered the pet store everyone turned around to find out where that awful stink was coming from. Tommy found the groomer and told her what happened. "I'm going back to clean out my truck" stated Tommy to the groomer.

A half an hour later, the groomer had Jack on his leash with a pretty blue bow around his neck. Tommy laughed when he saw Jacks look on his face. "Oh what a handsome boy" said Tommy. He pets him on his head as the pup just started to paw at the bow to get it off. "I used rose scented shampoo to get the smell out" stated the groomer. "Oh Jack you smell like a rose" teased Tommy.

The groomer waved after Tommy loaded him up into the truck and drove off. Jack laid down on the floor and with a few yanks finally got the bow off.

Tommy pulled over to the side of the road by a corn field. He climbed back into the bed area and talked to Jack. "I know you were trying to be nice by feeding those ducks. I still love you" then he gave the pup a big hug. "Now, let's put the hammer down and get this load of popcorn delivered" said Tommy. He pushed the air brake button and drove off to enter the highway once again.

Jack slept most of the ride and Tommy's truck wasn't stinky anymore it smelled like a rose bush instead. Finally, after a few more hours on the highway they got their load of popcorn delivered. The two truckers were happy to be on their way home for the weekend. Tommy thought *maybe Jack should stay home with Tammy during the next trip.* Yes, Tommy is married to a lady named Tammy. They have two grown children and two cats that Jack likes to cuddle with.

Just then, Tommy pulled his big rig into his long winding driveway and pulled the cord on the air horn. Wah Wah it sounded. Tommy jumped out and pulled out Jacks ramp to get him the heck out of his truck. Jack ran off into the house. Tammy stood in the doorway to greet them as they arrived. "What's his problem?" asked Tammy to Tommy. "Oh we had a mishap at the popcorn factory" replied Tommy.

"I'll pour you a cup of coffee then you can tell me all about it" said Tammy. The two sat down for a cup of coffee to catch up on the events that happened while Tommy was away. He told her about how Jack found an opened bag of cheese popcorn and fed it to the ducks and how the forklift driver landed in a pile of duck poop. "Sounds like he was a trouble maker on this trip" Said Tammy to Tommy.

Jack walked over to the table where everyone was sitting. He laid down on the floor so Tommy could rub his belly. Tommy gave Jack a pet on the head and whispered in his ear. "I wonder where we'll go next."

The End